the Beatles

dress rehearsal

I started my career in photography as assistant to Dezo Hoffmann. I learned an awful lot from Dezo about lighting and developing. I then decided to go freelance. The 'Our World' session was just one of the many I covered for The Beatles. Looking back at the photographs which I took on that summers day in 1967 I am staggered by their innocence, it is astonishing to see them again 30 years later. Sadly the shots I took of Brian Epstein at the 'Our World' session turned out to be the last ones ever taken of The Beatles and their manager together in public.

The first time I photographed The Beatles was at a concert they performed at a public school in Stowe in April 1963. It was a most unusual occasion. Since then I photographed them numerous times both in the studio and on tour between 1963 and 1967. I worked closely with NEMS and Tony Barrow and was involved with the Brian Epstein's stable of stars. It's only now after all these years you realise how fortunate you were to be there. It is difficult without sounding blasé but you would be sat in the office and all of a sudden Ringo Starr would come in and sit down and nobody would make a great fuss about it, it was just one of The Beatles........nice guys, they all used to wander in casually........Cilla, Gerry, Billy J. Kramer.

The incident that brought home to me what Beatlemania was all about was when we were in, I think, Denmark, and as I left the dressing room where I had been chatting with The Beatles a girl came up to me and said "I want to touch you" I asked "why?" and she replied "because you've been in the same room as one of The Beatles"........that was Beatlemania crystallised........that was the power of those guys.

The Beatles were professionals and they liked people who knew what they were doing, they did not suffer fools. They were pleasant and great fun to be with. Ringo was always humourous, always funny, always cracking a joke. John was a very quick witted man, he could be biting but he was very very bright with a sharp sense of humour. Paul had great charm and was a really warm person. George was probably the quietest in nature of all The Beatles, he was easy going and a great musician who cared about his music.

The Beatles 'Our World' recording session was relaxed and comfortable, they encouraged girl friends, close friends and fellow musicians to drop in, which was unusual as during other recording sessions I covered they liked to work alone in the studio with as few visitors as possible. The Beatles, like many other musicians when they were in the studio, would wander round and play with other instruments which may have been lying around, it was always fascinating to watch that. It was not that they wanted to do each others jobs, just maybe a bit of relaxation to get away from their own instrument.

Brian Epstein would sometimes drift in and out of a session, he wouldn't hang round, he would go back to the office do some work and maybe come back again later. His death came as a great shock. George Martin was a great calming influence in the studio. He would never say "I want you to do this or that," with him, everything was very gently done. It was a great team.

- David Magnus

David Magnus was born in 1944 and worked as Dezo Hoffman's assistant before becoming a freelance photographer. He has photographed most of the prominent bands of the 60's both in England and on location overseas. In addition to his work in the music business, David also worked widely in both the film and television industry before retiring three years ago. David now lives in London with his wife Janice and children.

r e h e a r s a l

It was in 1966 that the BBC had the idea of creating the first television show to be broadcast live around the world. It was to be a celebration of the recent huge advances in satellite communication and an opportunity to emphasise global unity.

The eventual concept, announced on May 18th 1967, was for the national broadcasting networks of 10 countries to each provide material for a live 125-minute transmission so that viewers would be able to watch live action in, for example, America followed by live action in Australia, Japan, Tunisia or Spain. Viewers in each participating country would see the pictures simultaneously.

Each contribution not only needed to capture the contemporary national mood but to be easily understood around the world. The Beatles were Britain's natural candidates and, after being approached, agreed to write a song for the event.

"A senior producer at the BBC Television came to us and explained that they were going to go from Canada to London to Tokyo in a massive global link-up," remembered Paul. "At first we thought it would be like the Eurovision Song Contest with lots of people hanging around but we were assured that it would be nothing like that. The technology had changed and the show would be seen by billions of people. We thought it would be a great opportunity to get our message over. It was quite an honour to be Britain's contribution."

The request came during one of The Beatles busiest recording schedules. Within the past six months they had recorded the singles 'Strawberry Fields Forever' and 'Penny Lane', the album 'Sgt. Pepper's Lonely Hearts Club Band' and were currently recording tracks for the 'Yellow Submarine' soundtrack.

The 'Sgt. Pepper' album, on the verge of being released at the time, had all but creatively exhausted the group. The tracks written for 'Yellow Submarine' were done grudgingly to fulfil an obligation and often sounded like it. They had done all their serious hard work on 'Sgt. Pepper' and now it was playtime. Songs like 'It's All Too Much', 'Hey Bulldog' and 'All Together Now' were appropriately reminiscent of playground chants and street rhymes. The last track recorded before the BBC session was 'You Know My Name (Look Up The Number)', a goofy jam of John's, reminiscent of the Bonzo Dog Doo Dah Band.

The one requirement for the 'Our World' broadcast, as it was now being called, was that The Beatles' song should be simple enough to be easily understood by the potential 500 million audience in 31 countries.

Legend has it that just as John and Paul used to compete for the A sides of singles so they competed for the 'Our World' show - Paul coming up with 'Your Mother Should Know', a nostalgic thirties style song which tipped its hat in the direction of his father Jim McCartney's pre-war dance band tastes, and John submitting 'All You Need Is Love', a number which pivoted on the chanting of the simple word 'love' and which had the slow tempo of a communal song,

If this scenario is true - and Brian Epstein's former NEMS assistant Tony Bramwell insists that it is - it's easy to see why John's song won out. Paul's was rooted in a specifically Western musical tradition and looked backwards. It may have sounded like a song Paul's mother would have known but not like the song that the mother of a young viewer in Bulgaria or Mexico would have known.

John's, on the other hand, contained the requisite simple words and looked forward to a time of universal harmony. For a show that was to celebrate the enhancement of international communications and a feeling of global cosiness it was the obvious choice.

To the world at large, 'All You Need Is Love' could either be taken as a call for world peace or a plea for romantic understanding. The Beatles, after all, had made their debut with 'Love Me Do' and had hit their high-spot as a scream inducing pop group with ' She Loves You' and 'Can't Buy Me Love'. Love, love, love and yeh, yeh, yeh, were the optimistic sounding words which clothed The Beatles in their prime.

But this was a different love, 'All You Need Is Love' added a playful reference to 'She Loves You' as it ended and it was meant to suggest a contrast just as their besuited dummies circa 1963 contrasted with the serious band musicians of 1967 in the cover photo for 'Sgt. Pepper'. It was their way of saying; 'This is where we were - this is where we are now'. They weren't mocking their earlier incarnations but letting us know that they had grown.

The catalyst for the change was undoubtably psychedelic drugs, LSD in particular. In a celebrated incident in the autumn of 1965 both John Lennon and George Harrison had unwittingly embarked on their first acid trip when a dentist friend spiked their after dinner coffees as a little farewell gift. It was to be the first of many trips and the drug was to leave an indelible mark on their artistry.

Masters and Houston in their landmark book 'The Varieties of Psychedelic Experience' (1966), reported that one of the characteristics of the LSD experience is a feeling that the subject is now full of a powerful and life-changing love. "This idea emerges that a universal or brotherly love is possible and constitutes man's best, if not only, hope."

It was certainly a belief that came to grip John and, after Paul's first experience with LSD in March 1967, he too would become a convert, explaining to a newspaper: "The need today is for people to come to their senses and my point is that LSD can help them. We all know what we would like to see in the world today - peace. We want to be able to get on with each other. I believe the drug could heal the world... I now believe that the answer to everything is love "

'Baby You're A Rich Man', the song chosen for the flip side of 'All You Need Is Love', continued the theme. You become a rich man, one of the beautiful people, when you partake of the secret knowledge. You know all there is to know and it's simply a matter of deciding how you're going to use this wisdom. George Harrison boasted that, for him, taking LSD was like gaining hundreds of years of experience within twelve hours, "It was like opening the door, really, and before that you didn't even know there was a door," he said. "It just opened up this whole other consciousness. I had such an overwhelming feeling of well-being, that there was a God, and I could see him in every blade of grass,"

The 'Our World' broadcast, although organised by those 'straight' people from television who would never have countenanced LSD consumption, encouraged a new global consciousness which complemented the acid head vision of a world where divisions were dissolved. It was a vision that would stay with John for the rest of his life. In one of his final interviews he said: "We're one world, one people, whether we like it or not. I mean, we can pretend we're divided into races and countries and we can carry on pretending that until we stop doing it, but the reality is that it is one world and it is one people."

This idea of universal love had already taken root in the emerging psychedelic counterculture, particularly in the Haight Ashbury area of San Francisco. Young people headed towards the city in 1967 believing that they would find alternative ways of living characterised by the 'gentle loving' of Scott McKenzie's hit single 'San Francisco (Be Sure To Wear Flowers In Your Hair)',

There had been a 'Human Be-In' held in Golden Gate Park in January where the Grateful Dead, Jefferson Airplane and Quicksilver Messenger Service had shared the stage with acid guru Timothy Leary, poet Allen Ginsberg and others. The press release announced that a "new concept of human relations" was being developed and that the Human Be-In was "the joyful, face-to-face beginning of the new epoch."

Although The Beatles had played San Francisco three times and the city's Candlestick Park had been the scene of the group's final concert in the summer of 1966, they had few opportunities to explore its subculture.

Paul was the first to visit, in April 1967. He ended up jamming with the Jefferson Airplane at their white mansion and returned full of enthusiasm for all that was happening there. John was affected by what he had been told about the city, so much so that for a time he was keen for The Beatles to re-locate to Haight Ashbury.

Love and peace were the buzz words of the year, featured (usually in rubbery psychedelic writing) on buttons and tee-shirts and symbolised by what Allen Ginsberg dubbed 'flower power'. In mass demonstrations against American involvement in the Vietnam War protesters would chant 'Make love, not war' . To journalists they became known as peaceniks, the Love Generation or the Flower Generation.

'All You Need Is Love' didn't create the movement but its perfect timing meant that it would become the song of youthful hope during a summer marred by war in Biafra, bombing raids on North Vietnam, race riots in Detroit and the aftermath of the six day Arab-Israeli war.

The 'Our World' broadcast on June 25th ostensibly showed The Beatles recording their long-awaited follow up single to 'Strawberry Fields Forever'/ 'Penny Lane' but of course nothing could be left to chance either for a new Beatles record or for a live show of such historical significance. This meant that much of the track was pre-recorded and John's live vocal would be re-recorded.

As George Martin later admitted; "It had to be kept terribly secret because the general idea was that the television viewers would actually see The Beatles at work recording their new single - although, modern recording being what it is, we obviously couldn't do that for real; so we laid down a basic rhythm track first of all."

Recording had started eleven days earlier at Olympic Studios in Barnes, south London, where The Rolling Stones had recently recorded 'Let's Spend The Night Together' and 'Ruby Tuesday'. Here they worked through the night with George Martin and engineer Eddie Kramer to produce a basic rhythm track. After five and a half hours during which they did 33 takes they had a rough mono mix featuring John on harpsichord, Paul on double bass, Ringo on drums and George on violin.

"John has an amazing thing with his timing," George Harrison later said of the music for the song. "He always comes across with very different time signatures. It just sort of skips a beat here and there and changes time. But when you question him as to what it is he's actually doing, he really doesn't know. He just does it naturally."

Paul made similar observations. "It was quite a strange little song, " he said. "It was a very good song but it had different time things all set against each other which made it quite complex until you came to the chorus which got you hooking away."

Tony Bramwell took an acetate of this very basic recording to Derek Burrell Davis, BBC Television's Head of Outside Broadcasting. He also took him a copy of an eight minute film that had been made during the recording of the Sgt. Pepper track 'A Day In The Life' as an example of what they wanted to do on the night.

"The Beatles wanted to show people having fun in the studio while they were recording," says Bramwell. " At first the BBC was worried. They didn't think it would be possible to have all these people in a recording studio and they were worried about people misbehaving. I assured them that everyone would be very responsible."

On June 19th they used Studio Three at EMI Studios, Abbey Road, to overdub vocals, drums, piano and banjo. Two days later a remix was completed for Burell Davis. On June 23rd an orchestra (four violins, two cellos, two tenor saxophones, two trombones, two trumpets, a flugelhorn and a piccolo trumpet) was brought in to record a number of overdubs.

The track had been arranged by George Martin ("a fairly arbitrary sort of arrangement since it was at such short notice...") and, in the spirit of the international occasion, he had added a quote from the French national anthem to introduce the song and snippets from Bach (Germany), Glen Miller (America) and Greensleeves (an English folk tune first mentioned in the 16th century) in the long play out.

Paul later remembered that there was trouble over the use of the excerpt from Glen Miller's 'In The Mood' because, unlike the other music, it was not yet out of copyright. "We thought of all the great clichés because they're a great bit of random," said Paul. "It was a hurried session, and we didn't mind giving George Martin that to do - saying, 'There's the end - we want it to go on and on'.

''Actually, what we wrote was much more disjointed. So when we put all the bits together we said 'Could we have 'Greensleeves' right on top of that little Bach thing? And on top of that we had 'In The Mood'."

On June 24th, the day before transmission, Abbey Road was opened to journalists and photographers during the morning and The Beatles posed with their balloons and 'love' placards. The afternoon was taken up with a camera rehearsal for The Beatles and the orchestra and the evening with recording overdubs.

"When everything was finished I went into the West End with The Beatles road manager Mal Evans to find people that we could ask along to the recording," says Tony Bramwell. "We went down to The Revolution, The Speakeasy, The Bag 'o' Nails and The Scotch of St. James and just asked people we knew to come along. No-one phoned each other in those days because everyone moved house so frequently and you were never sure where they lived."

It was only on this day that the final decision was made to release 'All You Need Is Love' as the Beatles next single. No track from 'Sgt. Pepper' was ever used as a single. "It is an inspired song and they really want to give the world a message," announced manager Brian Epstein. "The nice thing about it is that it cannot be misinterpreted. It is a clear message saying that love is everything."
On the day of the recording the Beatles arrived at the Abbey Road studios at 2.00pm and used the afternoon for another camera rehearsal in Studio One, scene of all their great recordings, where the evening session was to take place. An outside broadcast vehicle was parked in the studio forecourt.

For the recording, the studio was filled not only with The Beatles and orchestra musicians but with those friends they'd rounded up the night before: Mick Jagger, Magic Alex, The Fool, Keith Moon and his girlfriend, Eric Clapton, Graham Nash (Hollies), Gary Leeds (Walker Brothers), Pattie Harrison, Jane Asher, Marianne Faithfull, Mike McCartney and John Lennon's friend Terry Doran.

"We knew it was going to be an exciting evening," said Paul. "We'd worked on the song for a few days and knew what we were going to do. Then we piled all our friends into the studio. There was Mick and Eric Clapton and all the girls. We thought, well, if Britain's going to be waving hello to the world then we had better invite all our friends."

The party atmosphere was created with flowers, streamers and balloons (even though the BBC broadcast was only in black and white), placards bearing the song title in various languages and guests sitting cross-legged on the floor around the performers clapping along to the music.

The entire 'Our World' show was divided into sections each featuring a different aspect of human experience. The Beatles were to appear in the 'Artistic Excellence' section which would be narrated by heavyweight BBC anchorman Cliff Michelmore. They would be introduced by veteran British disc jockey Steve Race.

Due to some wrangling by communist bloc countries, the Soviet Union, Poland, East Germany, Czechoslovakia and Hungary pulled out at the last minute and were replaced by Denmark. Bulgaria, Romania and Yugoslavia, who were due to broadcast the programme without contributing, dropped the transmission as a result. All this probably cost 'Our World' around 150 million viewers.

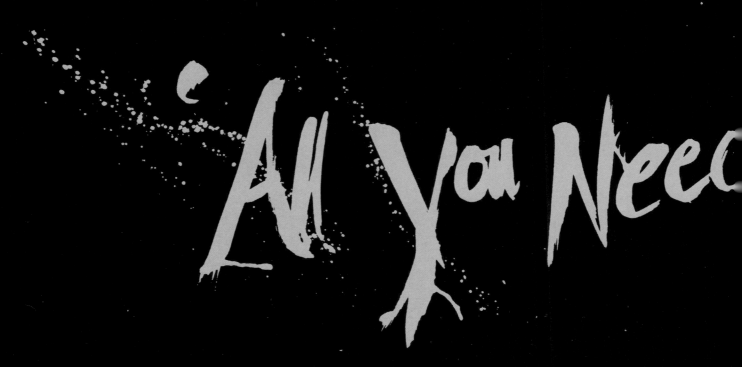

The Beatles went on air at 21:36 local time, performing to their rhythm track while Paul added bass, Ringo drums and George a guitar fill. The orchestra, wearing evening dress, performed live and the result, with a simultaneous mix by producer George Martin and engineer Geoff Emerick, was routed directly to the BBC van and from there to the Early Bird 'space booster' and ATSIB and Lani Bird satelites.

In this way viewers on five continents witnessed a preview of the next Beatles single and were left with the feeling that they were seeing history in the making. Ringo sat behind his drum kit with streamers dangling from his hair while John, Paul and George perched on high stools with flowers tucked in behind their headphones. Only Ringo and George now had their 'Sgt. Pepper' moustaches but all were wearing riotously coloured costumes designed especially for the occasion by The Fool.

The defining image of the 6 minute and 11 second appearance was that of John nonchalantly delivering his vocals while chewing gum and gripping the left ear of his head set. He made it look as though it was just another days work .

The Beatles had long perfected the art of taking the tension out of grand moments with a smirk but according to Richard Lush, the EMI tape operator for the day, the indifference during 'Our World' masked John's jitters.

"He was very nervous that day," said Lush. "He might not have looked it, but I was used to working with him and you get to know when someone is nervous." Later that night, after all the guests had departed, John re-recorded his vocal and didn't leave the studio until one the next morning.

The version of 'All You Need Is Love' that would be released on record received its final mix the day after the broadcast. Ron Pender, former EMI Studio engineer recalls, "The Beatles had decided to rush release 'All You Need is Love' as a single and I worked until late the day following the broadcast transferring the tracks to acetate. 'All You Need Is Love' had proved no problem but there were difficulties with 'Baby You're A Rich Man'. The technical guys had been experimenting with a new cutting amplifier. At that time the game was who could cut records the loudest and they were using a new amplifier capable of recording at much higher levels. But every time the clapping noises sounded on 'Baby You're A Rich Man' the waste swarf from the acetate would break and collect up around the cutting stylus and then catch fire! In the end we had to use one of the old cutting amplifiers." `All You Need Is Love' was released eleven days later on July 7th and rapidly went to the top of the singles charts in both Britain and America.

"We did it in a way to get over the message and it was right for the time," said George. "All the people who wanted to hear that sort of thing heard it, and all the people who thought it was a load of old cobblers still thought it was. It was harmless though, and it didn't kill anybody did it?"

When forced to articulate what the message of The Beatles was the group members would always mention something about love . Even when the group disbanded their individual concerns remained with issues of peace, justice and harmony whether it was Paul and his concern over animal welfare, George with his continuing involvement with the Krishna Consciousness movement or John in his campaigns against war.

"If we had anything to say to the world, then this would be it," said Paul after it was all over. "The song was a way of putting this philosophy over to everyone. We were told that we would be seen recording it by the whole world at the same time so we had one message for the world. Love. We need more love in the world."

- Steve Turner

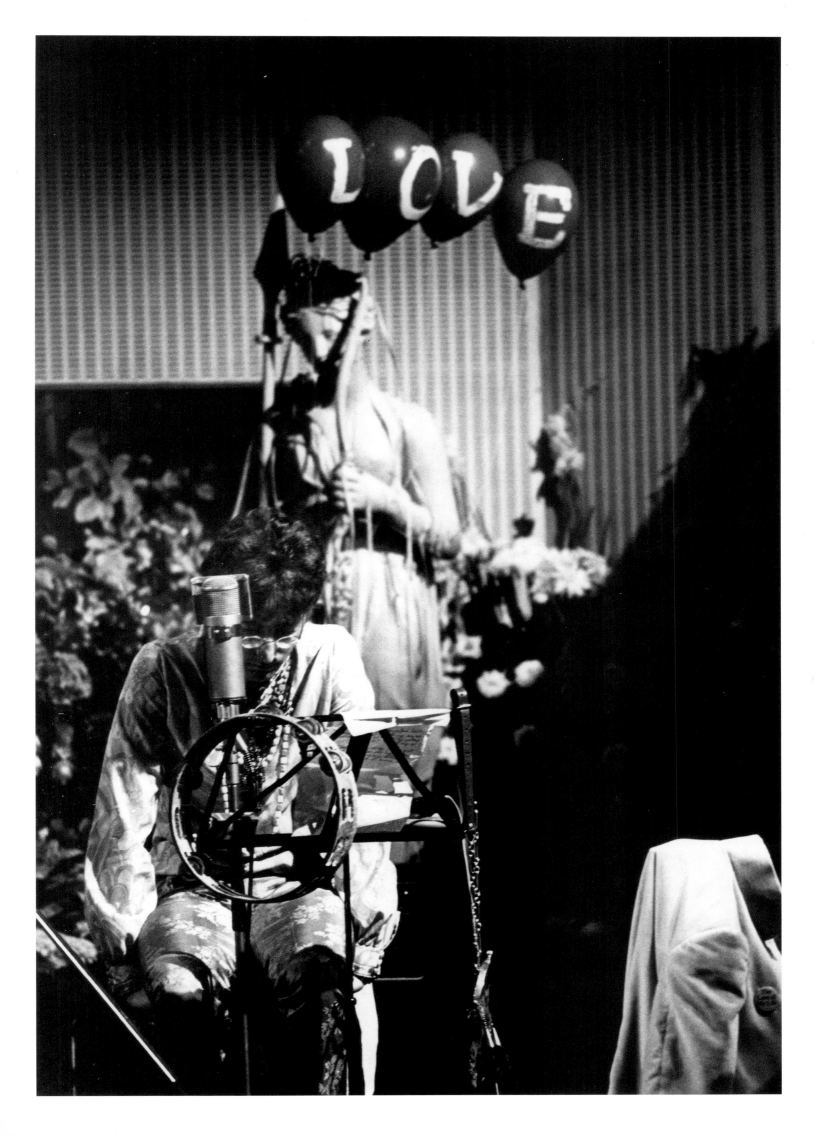

"He always comes across with very different time signatures. It just sort of skips a beat here and there and changes time. But when you question him as to what it is he's actually doing, he really doesn't know. He just does it naturally."

- George Harrison on John Lennon

"It is an inspired song and they really want to give the world a message."

- Brian Epstein.

April 29,97

Dear Jason Cornthwaite,

 Ta for the stats about All You Need is Love. I feel in my mind
I was there, can see it taking place, remember them
rehearsing the song,have read in Beatles ref books that I was
there- but alas I don't think I was. I can find no hard
evidence I was there. Vee strange.

 I have just looked in my 1967 diary.Haven't you kept yours ?
On June 22 I was with Mal and Neil from 2 till 8 in the
evening. Doesn't say where. Perhaps Abbey Road,or their homes.
On July 6 I was at Paul's for dinner, with Jane Asher. On
July 13 I was in New York. I interviewed U Thant in the
afternoon and saw Nat Weiss ,the Beatles US man,in the
evening.So my diary says.Next day I saw Sid Bernstein.

 I was working on the Beatles biog all this time, going to
Abbey Rd when they were rehearsing, or Paul's. I can remember
them rehearsing the song, but I'm just not sure if I was there
on the night of June 24.I do have my note books, where I made
notes of each interview,each event, but haven't time to look
through them - and anyway I can never read my handwriting. If
only I had taped all my interviews,wot a treasure I'd have.

 So anyways,that's all I can say.Best of luck with the book...

Yours
Hunter Davies

Hope you'll send me a copy of the book?

Hunter tries to set the record straight.

KODAK SAF.ETY FILM

"I'd already left the Manfreds by then and I was making a living as an arranger.
I'd done work on some of George Martin's projects so I knew him quite well.
Normally he'd have done all the arranging on something like All You Need Is Love
but he'd had such a bad week that he called me up and asked if I would do it.

We only had a few days to get it all organised. I was sent an acetate which consisted of a backing track for the song, played by The Beatles which included George Harrison playing a violin for some reason. The Marseillaise opening was already there, but there wasn't much else. My job was to come up with an orchestration for it.

I went up to Paul's house in Cavendish Avenue, and set to work with him and John in a room upstairs. Even though I'd been in quite a successful band, and had met them before, it was pretty awe-inspiring to be working with them. I was also very conscious that they had a great relationship with George Martin, and it wasn't easy to step into his shoes.

We had three days at Abbey Road. The first was a day purely of sound rehearsals, to let the orchestra have a look at what I'd done. You can imagine my horror then, when we were all gathered in the studio and my score didn't turn up. I'd sent it off to the copyist who copies out the parts for the individual players in the orchestra, and he'd done the work but he got caught in the taxi in some traffic on Park Lane. So there's me, on my first assignment with the world's most famous band and I was holding everything up. I felt awful.

The second day included some camera rehearsals as well as music. One thing I liked about working with them was they were very fluid. Nothing was set in stone. They had a basic idea, then worked on it as we went along. The idea to include Greensleeves and In The Mood as part of the orchestration came out as we went along.

The third day was great. We'd rehearsed everything by then so I felt fairly comfortable and I'd got myself a new suit from Take 6 specially for the occasion. I know that George Martin and Geoff Emerick were under a lot of pressure that day but I just enjoyed it. When the guests started turning up it turned almost into a party. Not a real party, mind you, but a studio that felt a bit like a party."

- Mike Vickers, ex-Manfred Mann, also
conducted the Our World orchestra.

Beatles take a Break

"We'd had an idea to do 'A Day In The Life' promo film which was to turn the orchestral recording session into a party. That film was made but never shown because the record was banned, but we used the basic format for the "All You Need Is Love" transmission. I went to the director, Derek Burrell Davis and said 'we want to have a party going on with the orchestra all there'.

The Head of the BBC was a nice chap, they always are, he was called Aubrey Singer. He just asked Brian, who asked the boys, and they said yes. With The Beatles, it was always if you asked them in a certain way to do something, they'd do it, but if you asked them in a negative way and said "you wouldn't like to do this" then they'd agree. They were asked in the right way and they were in the studios anyway having just finished Sgt. Pepper, and they started writing a few songs at the end of May. John had "All You Need Is Love" in a rough state, and Paul had a tune which was "Your Mother Should Know" demoed. They picked "All You Need Is Love". They recorded a version of it, not at EMI, but at Olympic Studios. George was playing violins, Paul was playing string bass and John was playing harpsichord.

I took this away the following day I think, and took it to the Beeb and played it to Aubrey Singer and Derek Burrell Davis, who was the director that had been nominated to put the thing together. I took along a copy of the film for "A Day in the Life", and sat at the viewing room at Television Centre and the director said "we can't possibly have anything like this going on", as it would interfere with the cameras and the sound equipment and everything. I said that it didn't on the day it was recorded and that was with a forty piece orchestra, we were only going to do overdubbing or miming with a 13 or 15 piece orchestra. They thought that it would get out of hand but agreed as long as there weren't any rough people there.

We'd had all the guests and friends there for "A Day in the Life", you see, so they could see what it was going to look like. I don't think that they understood who Mike Nesmith from the Monkees was, and it was also about the same time that The Stones were getting busted. I think the week before The Beatles carried on recording and nearly finished the whole recording of it. Then the day before we all went up to the studios for a press conference and The Beatles were wearing sandwich boards, and the big globe balloon and things like that George Martin was still doing mixes of it for the following day.

On the day before the broadcast it was the press conference thing in the morning, then the afternoon at the main studio in Abbey Road. We all went down to the Speakeasy in the evening and started finding people; "Here you, come up to the studios tomorrow!". It was planned with some people, but most of them we just met up with somewhere in town. You only had to go into the Speakeasy, the Cromwellian, the Bag of Nails and the Scotch of St James and you'd find nearly everyone in this party. "You know tomorrow 2 o'clock, EMI, be there". And that was sort of how it was.

We just chose the people we knew........Eric (Clapton) and his girlfriend, Mick (Jagger) and Marianne (Faithful) , Moony (Keith Moon). I remember Moony. We found him in the Speakeasy, he was absolutely enjoying himself, and throwing peanuts everywhere. We said that there was a party tomorrow night and he said; "Right, I'd better go home then", and his chauffeur took him home. Neville I think his name was. On the Sunday we got up there about lunch time, and Brian was there. We spent the time doing a few run-throughs and picking which actual mix was going to be used, and what was going to be over-dubbed live and what was going to be mimed to.

On the night it was a backing track that had been done the day before and there were some live vocals, John's mainly, and some of the musicians were live. Paul's "She Loves You" and those little bits, as well as the guy with the piccolo, Dave Mason. He played the same chords as on "Penny Lane" and on the same trumpet as well. I sort of stood at the back wearing one of those sandwich boards and then came in towards the end. They were also there for the press conference the day before; All You Need Is Love was written in lots of different languages on sandwich boards, as it was a world transmission.

The Beatles got a session fee for 'Our World', about a thousand pounds was the agreed sum from the BBC, I think, but it was mainly for the publicity. Then, when it came to the evening, everyone turned up and was given cheap BBC wine and sat around and joined in. It was all over very quickly.

People started arriving about half an hour beforehand, about six o'clock I think. I remember Mick because he had this beautiful painted coat on and Eric had just had his hair permed again. And The Fool, who were always colourful and silly, Simone and Marijke. Rosie Nash and Jennifer Eccles were there, she was always fun. And the drummer... Gary Leeds Walker (from Walker Bros) , he'd just had his hair permed too like Eric's, it was the thing to do that year because Jimi was just becoming big. The girls wanted to dance around, but they weren't allowed to as they would have got in the way of the camera and whatever, so everyone had to sit politely until the final choruses when everyone could join in. Everyone had bells on anyway so there was a lot of jangling and noises and hand clapping at the end. Nobody was difficult, only the EMI staff and the BBC technicians who were incapable of joining in with anything that was unexpected.

It was very archaic. EMI is phenomenal for filing; they've probably got paper-clips that The Beatles used filed away somewhere! Such a bureaucracy. Even if you've been to Abbey Road God knows how many bloody times the doorman still stops you and asks for your name, or "can you sign in?", even if you were a Beatle you were still stopped and asked to sign in and out. Everything had to be signed and budgeted for. We spent about £20 too much on the videos and we got told off. Each video cost less than £100 each.

The day went by without any major problems, apart from choosing which take to use, which I don't think was the same take that came out on the record the following week. I think that John went in and did some more overdubs and changed things around during the week because in those days you could get records out within seven days without any problem. It was only the day after that it was decided to make it into a single.

Paul had spent a lot of time learning instruments, he was such a capable musician, he could do everything himself anyway. Ringo and George didn't like being told what to do! Ringo was the drummer and he didn't see why Paul should interfere with his drumming, and George was the same with his lead guitaring; Paul was the bass player.

George had spent a lot of time working with other musicians, he'd been to India so he was experimenting with other stuff. John was experimenting with different sounds and they were all capable of doing nearly everything themselves. For most of the sessions they were just coming in as required, or if required at all. Not particularly on "Pepper", it was after that, definitely on the "White Album", I mean they were dragging themselves into the studio.

The atmosphere on the transmission day was very, very good. John was in a great mood. I can remember they all went on a big shopping expedition a few days before to get some fun clothes, John was particularly pleased with his jacket with the big sunflower on. I'm not sure that he wore it on the actual thing. Yeah, they were all in a great mood; they knew that the song was close to brilliant, but they weren't sure what to do with it.

All the guests appeared to enjoy it. There was a run through beforehand up until about five o'clock and just before the transmission actually started, so that everyone knew when to join in and when to behave themselves.

Everyone sat down where the gear was set up, under Paul's feet! Keith sat next to Ringo, then everyone else tried to sit next to John, as he was the vocalist, and he was likely to get the best shots. I think that Mick was a bit embarrassed by being there because The Stones were trying to do their album at the same time, ("Their Satanic Majesty's Request"), and he was seen as being at the beck and call of The Beatles.

George Martin just stayed in the control room with Geoff Emerick, and he was wearing a white suit. It was very exciting for him. He's a very calm man, I don't think that I ever saw George flustered, only occasionally when they were smoking dope in the studio would he say, "boys you can't do that because its not you that will get in trouble it's EMI". He was worried about the repercussions of that."

-Tony Bramwell, former head of Apple Promotions.

"It was quite a strange little song." - Paul McCartney

"We did it in a

way to get over

the message and

it was right for

the time"

-George Harrison

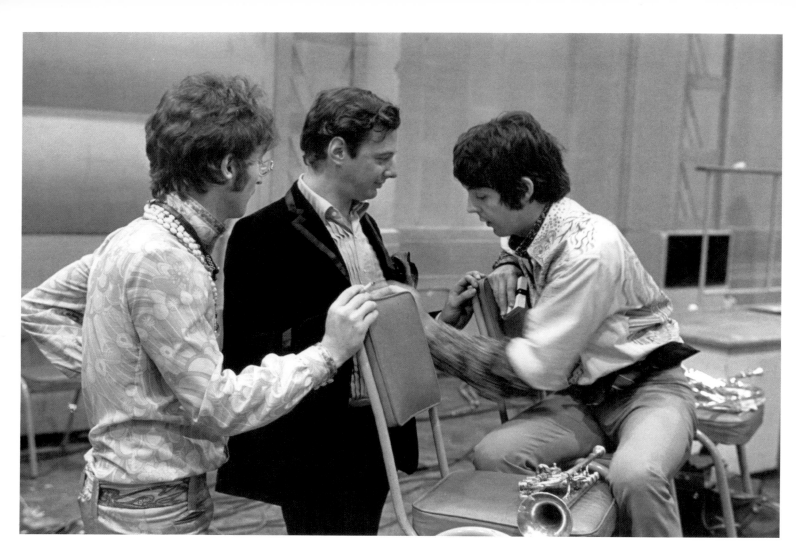

Paul sends out a message to his Aunt Milly in Australia.

"My wife, Joan, and I were watching with the family in Los Angeles around mid-day. Brian Epstein had telephoned from the studios to make sure we were tuned in to the Los Angeles educational channel. He told us "The boys' song is just beyond belief, quite the loveliest thing they've done. And absolutely the right message."

- Derek Taylor (Beatles publicist)

"It had to be kept terribly
secret because the
general idea was that the
television viewers would
actually see The Beatles
at work recording their
new single - although,
modern recording being
what it is, we obviously
couldn't do that for real;
so we laid down a basic
rhythm track first of all."

- George Martin

and friends

One day in the spring of 1967 I had a phone call from the BBCtv producer Derek Burrell-Davis "Would you like to spend a weekend at EMI Studios with The Beatles, while they make their next record?" he asked. I said I would. But what was the occasion?

As everyone now knows, it turned out to be part of an extraordinary historical and technical achievement: the first live worldwide television link, involving contributions from eighteen nations across the globe under the title 'Our World'. Two of the sequences would represent Britain, the first a report on the new town of Cumbernauld by Magnus Magnusson; the second my report from Studio 1 at Abbey Road in London describing how The Beatles were putting together their latest mega-hit. The total TV audience was estimated at five hundred million, spread across 31 countries. It was a colossal undertaking, not least in international switching control and timing. The programme began with the birth of a baby in Tokyo. What sort of world would the baby be entering? (And - the producers must have wondered, as they hopefully cued the mother - precisely when?)

On June 23rd I drove to the EMI Studios, which I knew well, being a contract Parlophone artist myself (George Martin was my A & R man too). Taking care to observe the Abbey Road pedestrian crossing, I went to the first floor studio where the preparatory tracks were to be laid down. There I greeted George Martin and was introduced by him to the four most famous people on earth.

John Lennon, slightly stocky in build, was preoccupied writing out words on a large scrap pad. Paul McCartney, alert and slightly cocky, was gently needling George Martin, who in his turn was sitting at the piano keyboard sketching out string parts for the forthcoming band rehearsal. George Harrison, dark and withdrawn, was fingering chords and doodling melodic figures on his guitar. Ringo Starr was sitting on a chair at the far side of the studio, seemingly happy in a drummer's world of his own. I sensed that the foursome were greeting me with a mixture of affability and slight reserve. Would I fawn over them? Was I going to play the heavy older musician? After all, they were in their early twenties; I was 46 and in no sense a rocker, as they well knew. Was I a friend? Yes, I was. And an admirer, too.

Paul seemed to be the accepted leader. He and George Martin were discussing the instrumental side of "All You Need is Love" and had already decided on the Marseillaise introduction (though for what reason I never discovered). Paul was suggesting bits of music for a final fade-out sequence based on the successful Sgt. Pepper model. "Perhaps a touch of Bach? How about Greensleeves? And what's that big band number that goes Da-deda-dah-dah...?" 'That number' turned out to be the standard intro to In The Mood, though I guessed there might be trouble later over the use of a composition that was still in copyright. After one of McCartney's suggestions George Martin said quite sharply "Don't be silly, Paul". Paul took the put-down without a murmur.

The following day we moved into the huge subterranean Studio 1 at the back of the EMI building. My 'narration suite' was a kind of garden shed with windows, normally used to isolate singers from the spill-over sound of their accompanying orchestras. In it I had a monitor screen, a microphone on a reading desk and a system of complicated cuelights. I put on what were known in the trade as 'split cans', earphones with one side devoted to the producer's instructions and the other to the overall studio sound. As the four Beatles arrived, Paul put his head round my door. "Hello again," he said, "how are you?", adding rather incongruously, "Lady Barnett- two marks." It was a reference to the radio panel game "Many A Slip", for which at the time I was co-question master with Roy Plumley. It surprised me that Paul should even be aware of Radio 4, until I reflected that The Beatles' lives were so restricted that they probably spent hours shut in hotels and dressing rooms with nothing much to do but listen to the radio, even Radio 4. You can't listen to Radio 1 all the time - as millions have since proved.

I settled down to work on my commentary, while the inevitable tedium of technical television rehearsals dragged on through the long afternoon. Every now and then I wandered out into the main studio for a brief chat with Paul or John - less with George who seemed somehow detached in a mini-world of his own. Again Ringo sat alone at the back, isolated but happy. "Boring, isn't it?" I remarked to George. He smiled and nodded in agreement - life for a Beatle wasn't always exciting. Meanwhile the various recorded tracks were being gradually built up under George Martin's expert guidance. In the car park Derek Burrell-Davis and his technical staff sweltered in the Outside Broadcast control van. It was midsummer's day. Making history can be a tedious business.

"The BBC want a live trail", Derek told me suddenly over my intercom. No one knew this had been planned, in fact to this day few people seem to know that such a promotion ever took place. The TV announcer told the viewers "Before we join the Black & White Minstrel Show here's Steve Race", and on cue I described what the sequence of events would be in Our World. The four Beatles had been assembled on a sort of fountain in the middle of the studio, and as I joined them they greeted me with a cheer. It was a derisive cheer, though I think a friendly one. I had a few words with each of them in turn. What was the song called? Whose idea had it been? ("His", they said, pointing to each other). And then I put the question to John that was intriguing me. Ninety five percent of all popular music is in 4-time, but there was more than a hint of unfamiliar 7-time in "All You Need Is Love". "Did you know your song was in 7-time?" I asked. I still remember the cool, serious look he gave me as he replied "Yes, I know". Then he indicated Paul, adding "- but blame him". Paul himself, alert as ever, noticed how, against my own instincts, I was trying to inject some breezy gaiety into the proceedings. He spoke encouragingly in my ear. "Yock it up, Steve ! " he said. He knew that it was my preference to be in the narrator's box doing a technical job, rather than "yocking it up". I duly yocked.

On Sunday June 25th the hard day's night began at 2 p.m. and was officially scheduled to end at 10 p.m. By now the studio was piled high with mountainous displays of flowers and balloons. John, Paul, George and Ringo climbed into their garish psychedelic outfits. The TV cameramen cursed as they cannoned into the floral displays that hampered their tracking lines. Mike Vickers' orchestral musicians came in for a first rehearsal; classical session men, of course, since rockers, however sympathetic, couldn't be trusted to read the music at sight. Leaving their instruments beside their chairs, the musicians went for a canteen meal break, where upon The Beatles posed with horn, Bach trumpet, and anything else that would please the photographers.

I dashed home to Wembley Park to collect my daughter Nicola. (I had named a composition of mine after her, and she and I had both been pleased when it won the Instrumental of the Year Ivor Novello Award). We were even more pleased when Paul looked in at the door of the narrator's booth to say hello. "Paul," I said, "this is my daughter Nicola". "Ah yes!" he replied. "La-LA-la la la la-la la ...." humming the first few bars of my tune.

The atmosphere was growing palpably more exciting. I stood and watched as the studio filled up with rock stars including Marianne Faithfull and Mick Jagger. As well as managerial types like Brian Epstein, there were general hangers-on and droves of flower-toting teenagers whom no one could remember inviting. They included some of the most beautiful girls I have ever seen in my life. The most rivetingly pretty turned out to be Pattie Harrison.

When the live "Our World" transmission had been completed, Derek Burrell-Davis thanked everybody officially, but the party celebrations carried on into the night. In the end, I went to say goodbye to each of The Beatles in turn and asked them to sign the front page of my TV script as a souvenir of a memorable occasion. Paul, jokey to the last and wrily amused that I was the one with the shortened name while his was unshortenable, wrote "To Stevie - Paul James McCartney". He was the only person who ever called me that. "Thank you, James" I replied.
I also went to say goodbye to Brian Epstein, who was enjoying himself wielding an enormous sword - or was it a sabre? - that he had brought along as his contribution to the fun. I never saw him again; he died two months later following a drug overdose.

On the way home in the car I noticed that my daughter was unusually silent. I think she was quietly fancying Paul McCartney. (I suspect she still does). As for me, I was singing over and over again "Love is all you need ... Love is all you need . . Love is all you need .." Well it's that kind of song, isn't it? And even now, thirty years later, I doubt if I'll ever get it out of my mind.

I'm not sure I even want to.

- Steve Race O.B.E Former BBC disc jockey
and 'Our World' narrator

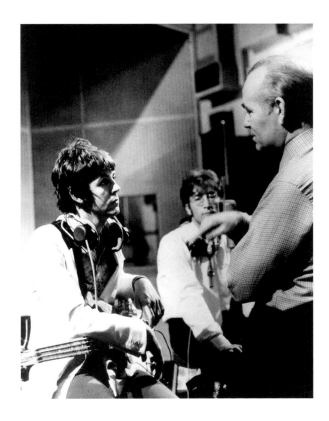

Steve Race chats with Paul and John in Abbey Road on Saturday 24 June 1967

"It was one of the great occasions of '67, it was the world's first biggest ever live T.V. show and Britain's contribution was The Beatles. They would be doing 'All You Need Is Love'.... and it was going to be a great party night, we were going to have a symphony orchestra who were all made to put on red plastic noses, and everybody was going to be there. The Rolling Stones would be there. The boys had to be at Abbey Road early for rehearsals and camera angles. Paul had asked me to pick up Jane from Cavendish Avenue, he said "It's party time Al!". So I went out and I bought a bright orange shirt, which was strictly against 'the man in the suit with the shiny shoes' image that I always had. I put on this bright orange shirt and got the car to pick me up and went up to Cavendish Avenue to collect Jane. She greeted me with the news "Oh Paul's bought you a shirt" so I said "What's wrong with the one I'm wearing?" Jane replied "It's alright but he wants you to wear this one" and she produced this multi-coloured silk shirt, a beautiful shirt, and it was all sort of splashed over with red, orange, green and yellow. I went to the bathroom to put this shirt on and then off we went to Abbey Road.

I arrived at the studio at around noon and did my usual tasks of supplying large quantities of cigarettes. They were always scrounging ciggies. Brian arrived at around 2pm. I had forgotten how ill Brian looked. Maybe I had not noticed at the time. But the photos show him looking slightly scruffy, certainly less than his usual immaculate self. At this time he was taking tablets to wake up and tablets to go to sleep. Only six weeks later Brian was dead.

The boys decided that I should carry one of the sandwich boards, which I wasn't very thrilled about but, you know, if they wanted you to do something you did it. My assistant, Tony Bramwell, was also grabbed to carry one and two other people whom I can't quite remember.

As the afternoon wore on, John became very tetchy and he kept disappearing to the toilet. Paul kept ribbing John about his nerves. It was all light hearted but John was not amused. All he could think about was singing live in front of 400,000,000 people. I stood talking to Brian when John walked over. "Brian I'm losing my voice" he croaked, we both laughed. We thought John was being daft but he was deadly serious. Paul didn't help by taking the mickey. By now we were only half an hour away from the live broadcast. "I can't do it Brian. I can't do it", John kept whispering. I dashed off looking for a drink for John or something which would ease his throat but Paul thought he was being a little "precious" and said so. "Come On John. Its only another gig" he said. "Just imagine you're singing for our friends here". It worked. Lennon chewed away on his gum and he was just brilliant."

- Alistair Taylor. Ex -NEMS and Apple employee , 'Mr Fix-it'

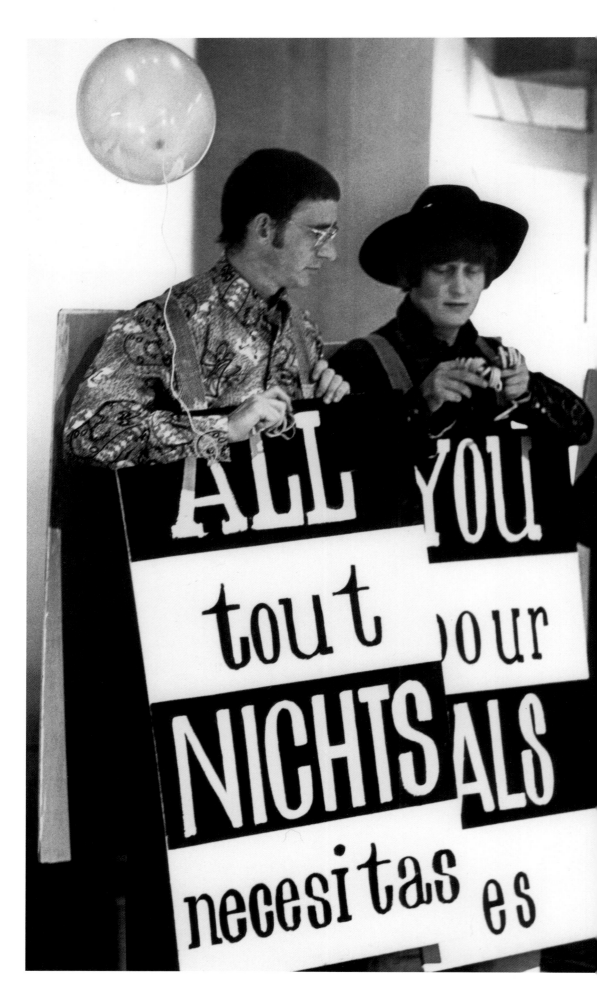

Alistair Taylor, on the left, wearing his present from a Beatle.

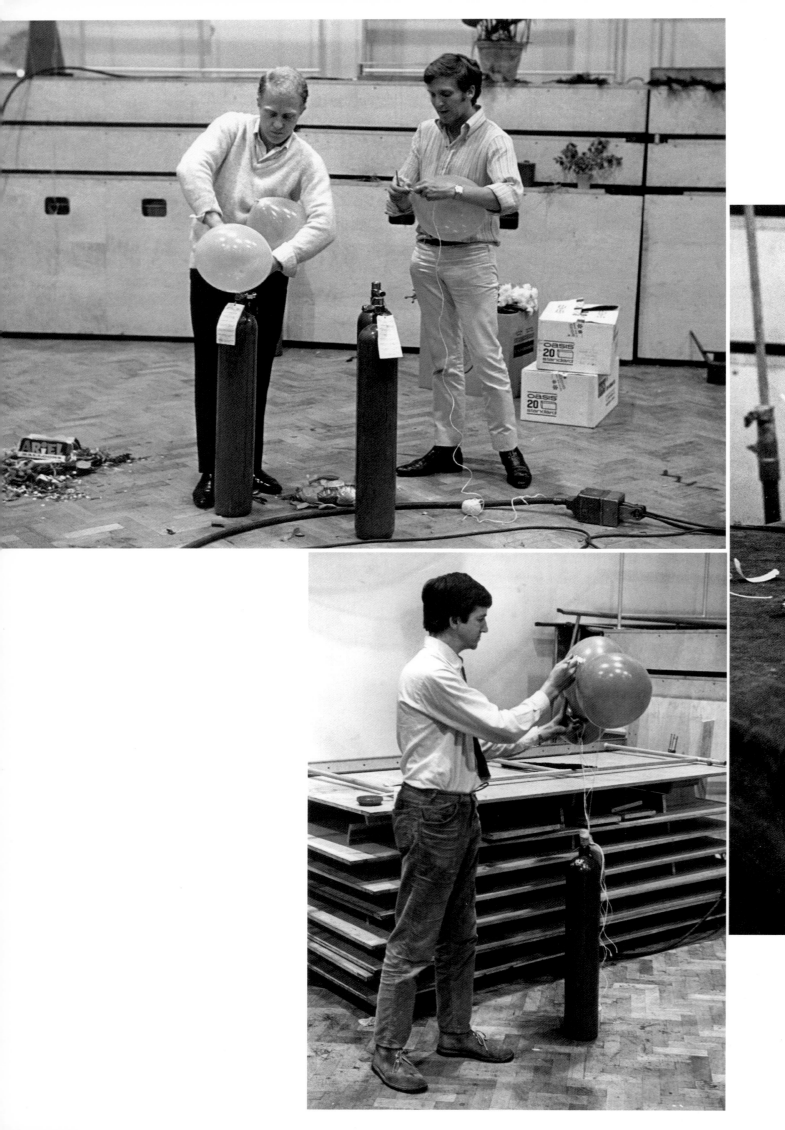

"Brian Epstein addressed us in his usual pompous style: 'It's all absolutely confidential and not one of us must utter a single word outside these four walls, but The Beatles are going to give a most important live performance next month." It was the second week of May 1967. I remember the date because it was my birthday. 'Eppy' had gathered together a handful of his executives who worked closely with the Fab Four in the largest office at NEMS Enterprises for what we were told would be a significant announcement.

The Beatles manager continued grandly "At the invitation of the BBC and the European Broadcasting Union. The boys are going to sing their latest song for a global audience of hundreds of millions, the largest number of viewers in television history, and it'll be a live broadcast from Abbey Road. They're to represent Britain in the first world-wide satellite link up." Someone asked what the new song was called and Brian replied tersely "I haven't the least idea. They haven't written it as yet as far as I know."

Although Paul did write something he felt was very suitable and George made some effort to do so it was John who came up with 'All You Need Is Love'. The very first time he played it to me and several others on a piano at Abbey Road. I could tell it was exactly right for 'Our World'. It carried a universal message which could not have been simpler and it was a repetitive chant which could be picked up very easily even by people who couldn't speak or understand the English language.

When George Martin listened to the first basic keyboard version of John's new composition, he immediately said 'We're making this the fastest rush-release job The Beatles have ever done - a single in the shops within days of the broadcast, availability worldwide almost simultaneously." We were all most impressed.

EMI Records and the BBC assumed responsibility for all the crucial technical arrangements for the 'Our World' event, but it fell to The Beatles own office to make a host of peripheral plans. Everyone at NEMS became involved to a greater or less extent, and the event was given top priority. Paul pointed out: "Even if we're very successful in generating a party mood on the record, we're left with an obvious problem. This is television, and a recording studio is not an exciting place visually. It's all got to look like the world's biggest party. We need hundreds of balloons, miles of party streamers and colourful bunting. Most of all, people must turn up in bright outrageous costumes, shiny silk shirts with multi-coloured designs, smocks and frocks with loads of flowers on them, chunky jewellery - the full works!"

Both Paul and his girlfriend, actress Jane Asher, joined in the 'hands-on' arranging, using their little black books to phone famous friends and convey invitations personally."

- Tony Barrow, The Beatles former press officer, 1963-68'

"We were all invited to a press call at Abbey Road on the day before the broadcast. There must have been well over a hundred press people there, because anything involving The Beatles was big news. We all milled around outside for a bit, I think. George was a bit late getting there, he'd been held up in traffic, but after he arrived they all put on these sandwich boards with "All You Need Is Love" written in different languages, which were used again the next day for the broadcast, and posed for the photographers.

George had on a brilliant orange jacket, Ringo was in a typically hippy yellow Afghan-type thing, but John and Paul were a bit more conservatively dressed. I remember somebody gave out some statistics about how there were 6,500 tv staff and 1,000,000 miles of cable involved in the broadcast, but what was more important to me was that I managed to get a quick word with each of them, because I knew them quite well from other occasions, such as when I'd gone on tour with them once.

Paul had just bought his farm in Mull Of Kintyre, which he got very cheap. I think he was looking to have somewhere he could get away from the glare of publicity all the time. I was kidding him on that he'd look great in a kilt, but he said he hadn't bought one yet. There was a rumour flying around that he was leaving the group, and he denied that. He was always the one who'd give you the most time.

John was a more abrupt, nervous type, given to shouting orders at everybody. I remember he told me that "All You Need Is Love" would be their next single, which even at that point still hadn't been announced publicly. George told me something about a tv show they had planned, which must have been "Magical Mystery Tour", and Ringo just talked about his garden, and some building work he was having done at home."

- Andy Gray, NME journalist.

'I was a background viewer that day because it was a very high-pressure event. Not only was it The Beatles performing live but it was being broadcast to some 300 million people around the world. It was the first major international satellite broadcast, so you had to be on the ball that day. I was very happy to be in the background and watch everyone else worrying.

It was a magical occasion, with all those guests.

Most of the rehearsal day was spent getting the orchestra right, The Beatles backing track was already recorded. The Beatles sang, and the orchestra rehearsed to the backing track. It was a chaotic day because as well as all the guests, the band and the orchestra we had all the television people there too, and it was the early days of colour television, remember. We weren't used to colour television, and the heat from the lights was far greater than you find in a modern television broadcast.

The guests weren't there during the rehearsal. They just turned up in No1 studio immediately before the broadcast and it turned into a party."

Peter Vince, (Abbey Road Studio engineer.)

"It was a great laugh, very nice. Fab!" - Mick Jagger
  commenting on the `Our World' broadcast

world

"We designed the costumes for the All You Need Is Love special, which was held at the height of the flower power thing. Nice piece of film, you can even see us sitting there. Brian Epstein tried to get me to carry one of the sandwich boards but I told him it wasn't my job!

The Fool were also commissioned to design the centre spread for the Sgt. Pepper sleeve but The Beatles didn't use it. That was basically a printing error. I think it was Paul who was supposed to have gone to the printer's, but he went off for the weekend, and they printed the wrong picture. By the time he came back they had about a million on the shelf so they left it like that.

John was just as committed as Paul to the idea of Apple, I remember John remarking, in an mild scouse accent, "I Love Barry and his dreams........and I'll buy the paint." - Barry Finch, The Fool.

"Our involvement with The Beatles initially started when Barry was representing Brian Epstein as a public relations man and had been asked to find an artist to do the design for the Savile Theatre which Brian owned. Barry liked Marijke's artwork, checked around, got a hold of her and Simon. He became friends with them, and Marijke and I used to get together when they were doing costumes for launching The Cream and for The Hollies and that sort of thing.

Barry took Simon and Marijke out of Bayswater and put them in a very nice apartment on Montague Square, right around the comer from Baker Street, where the Apple building was. All very convenient. The Beatles used to come round frequently. First it was the girls. Pattie came around quite a bit and she brought George. And finally we were asked to do some costumes and out of that came the idea for Apple.

It wasn't easy to enter The Beatles circle, it took months, actually. We often tried to make Simon and Marijke realise what a privilege it was. When you're young and arrogant you take it all for granted and think you're equally as great as they are. Maybe in our field we were, but The Beatles had a definite hold on the world. A phenomenon." - Josje Leeger, The Fool

I originally thought of the name 'The Fool' for us. Marijke and I were asked by George to design the fireplace at his Esher home and we spent 24 hours alone in the room creating this fabulous design. We also painted John's piano at his home in Weybridge - the first song he wrote on this was 'I Am The Walrus'. Also Marijke and I were responsible for designing the large mural on the outside of the Apple building in Baker Street. We employed about eight students to fill in all the colours. Towards the end of 1967 we all wanted to get away from England and go to New York. - Simon Posthuma, The Fool.

"I stayed up all night the night before. I didn't mean to, but I was drawing on a shirt. I had these pen things that you used to draw with and the ink didn't wash out. I stayed up all night doing it, and the shirt was nicked the next day."

- Paul McCartney

"At first we thought it would be like the Eurovision Song Contest with lots of people hanging around but we were assured that it would be nothing like that. The technology had changed and the show would be seen by billions of people. We thought it would be a great opportunity to get our message over. It was quite an honour to be Britain's contribution. "

- Paul McCartney

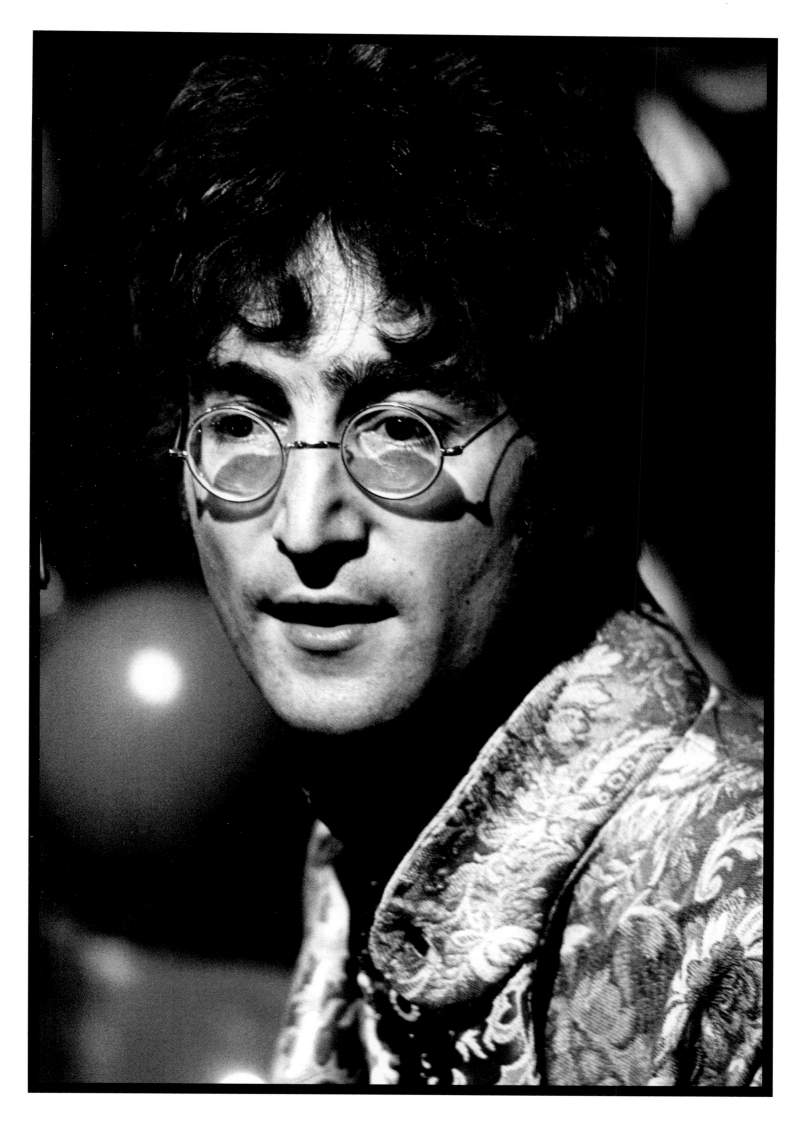

"It was for Love.... Love

and peace again. It was

a fabulous time"

- Ringo Starr

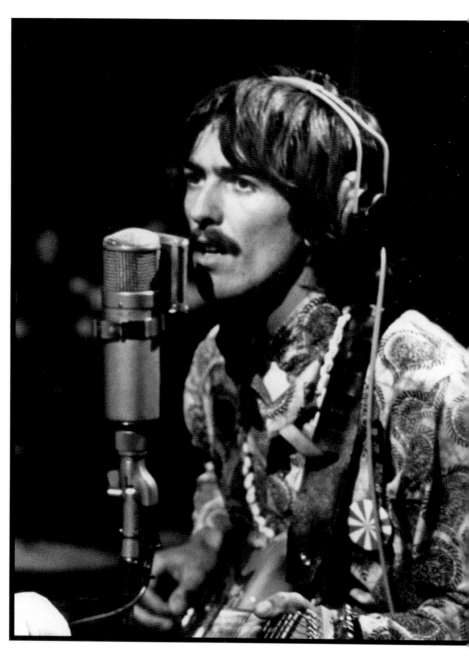

"We actually went on the air about forty seconds early. George (Martin) and I were having a welcome shot of Scotch whisky when we got the word over the intercome. There was a big panic to hide the bottle and the glasses. We were shoving them under the mixing console!"

- Geoff Emerick (Abbey Road Engineer)

"We played bits of Bach's Brandenburg Concerto in the fade-out." - Dave Mason, trumpeter

8

"We had one message for the world ...... love."

- Paul McCartney

'All You Need Is Love'

The Beatles Dress Rehearsal

T R A © K S

Fully illustrated Beatles catalogue available from:
Tracks Ltd, PO Box 117, Chorley
Lancashire, PR7 2QZ, England

Tel: 01257 269726
Fax 01257 231340
E-MAIL: SALES@TRACKS.CO.UK
Please visit our Beatles website: HTTP://WWW.TRACKS.CO.UK

Cat No. Tracksbe1
ISBN 1 898442 09 6